PowerHiking

Paris

*Eleven Great Hikes
Through the Streets of Paris
and Environs*

CAROLYN HANSEN   CATHLEEN PECK

Art direction and design	Dennis Gallagher and John Sullivan
	Visual Strategies, San Francisco
Title page illustration	Ron Rick
Map design	Ron Rick Designs
Maps	Ron Rick and Mike Kimball
Photography	Carolyn Hansen
Copy Editor	George Marsh
Additional photos	Katherine Neilsen, Lou Muckerman and photo stock
Printer	NORCAL Printing, San Francisco
Publishers	PowerHiking Ltd.

FOREWARD

This book will make your next trip to Paris more fun. If you have not yet been to Paris, it will give you some great ideas for how to spend your time in the City of Light. The book is especially written for travelers who want to see and experience everything, while getting some exercise too. If you *PowerHike*, then you can sample all of the fabulous French food and not worry. In Paris, food is always important.

Although we have walked every *PowerHike* several times and carefully recorded distances and times on a GPS device as we went along, there may be some slight variations as you do the hikes. Everyone walks at a different pace and everyone will spend more or less time exploring certain areas of interest. The names of stores and cafés may also change some-what. For the most part, however, the heart of Paris remains timeless. Any mistakes in the directions or the maps are ours, and we hope you forgive small inaccuracies.

We wish to thank our Power Partners, John and Rodney, without whose support we could not have gone forward. There are many friends and colleagues to thank as well. Ron Rick made our experience take shape on paper. Lindsey Crittenden and Janice Anderson-Gram generously took time to point us in the right direction. Our fellow hikers made our hikes an experience of fun and laughter. John Sullivan and Dennis Gallagher took us by the hand and made our project a reality.

—*Carolyn Hansen, Cathleen Peck*

WHAT IS POWER HIKING?

PowerHiking in Paris? Where would you hike? Where are the trails? What is *PowerHiking*? Paris is a city full of energy and action ready to be explored. It is a city perfect for *PowerHiking*! You want to see and do everything in the time you have available, and enjoy the marvelous French food and wine. You want to do it all. You want to *PowerHike*!

Paris is a hiker's dream. It has everything you could want—stunning views, exciting destinations, fascinating history, and varied terrain. At the end of each hike you have a sense of exhilaration and accomplishment because, not only have you walked everywhere, but you have also immersed yourself in history, art, and beauty. *PowerHiking* takes sightseeing to a new level of energy and interest. It is walking with a purpose that excites not only your senses but also your spirit. A day's *PowerHike* includes exercise, cultural sites, parks, gardens, museums, shops and cafes. Your days are full and, along with enjoying the celebrated French cuisine, you have also enjoyed French culture and beauty.

For *PowerHiking* you need comfortable walking shoes, layered clothing for changes

in the weather, and a carry-all or small backpack for your water, camera, and this book! Paris is a sophisticated city and you may want to dress more conservatively than when visiting a U.S. national park.

For example, urban walking shoes instead of hiking boots, pants instead of shorts, shirts instead of t-shirts, and no sweat pants. This way you can feel appropriately dressed for stopping in non-touristy cafes for lunch, or a chic boutique for some casual shopping.

This book is organized by neighborhood and the proximity of popular destinations within each neighborhood. For convenience each hike starts from the Carrousel entrance to the Louvre on the rue de Rivoli. This starting point leads to all the neighborhoods, as well as the metro and trains for adventures outside of Paris.

Put on your *PowerHiking* shoes, take a bottle of water, and head out for your first *PowerHiking* in Paris!

THINGS TO KNOW, BEFORE YOU GO

YOUR "LOOK" IN PARIS

How one is dressed is very important to Parisians. Adjust your "look" a little with stylish shoes, subtle-colored clothing (black is very practical and chic), and throw on a scarf or costume jewelry for pizzazz.

THE UNEXPECTED SITUATION

Part of the fun of traveling to different countries is the unexpected situations you encounter. An example is the time our friend visited "les toilettes" in a café, locked the door, and the lights went out. The light switch, outside the toilet, was on a timer and turned off the light automatically. She told herself not to panic, felt around for the door lock and escaped! We laughed until tears ran down our faces!

TAXIS

In Paris, taxis do not stop when you try to flag them down. There are taxi stands where they line up, in front of hotels, theatres, tourist destinations, and train stations. Otherwise, become familiar with the very practical and economical metro.

SCAMS

Pickpockets are plentiful in Paris. Keep your possessions under tight control, and do not be taken in by diversionary tactics. Also, do not be fooled by people (usually women) who beg on the street. The French government supports all services for the poor, and begging is a scam in which women and children are used to pull on the heartstrings of tourists.

CAFÉ/RESTAURANT DETAILS

If you want ice you must ask for it. The tip is almost always included in a 15% –18% service charge on your bill. You may leave a little extra if the service is notably good. Reservations are a necessity for good restaurants—ask your concierge to make one for you, securing a good table location.

CREDIT CARD DENIALS

It is becoming common for credit card issuers to deny charges when you travel outside the US because your previous spending pattern is only in the US. If you do not want to risk embarrassment when shopping, call the credit card issuer before you leave to advise them of your trip. This policy is meant to protect you from fraud.

SHOPPING AND CARRYING HOME

Shopping in Paris for gifts to bring home entails planning how to get them back. If your suitcase has a little room, flat, small items are perfect. If, however, you crave a Baccarat crystal vase, have the store ship it to you. They insure it, and you do not have to carry it back. Do not forget to ask for the VAT refund on purchases of 175 euros or more, made in one store on one day. To obtain the VAT refund (the steep sales tax paid by French residents), keep your purchases available for inspection at the VAT window at the airport. Remember: you cannot carry on liquids or cosmetics over the 3-ounce limit required by airport security. Go to the VAT window before checking your luggage, then check any liquids through.

POLITENESS

French people value politeness. Use the French you know, even if only "Bonjour," said with a smile. If they speak to you in English, do not be offended, but allow them to show their proficiency. When entering a shop or restaurant, make eye contact, smile, and say "Bonjour Madame" or "Bonjour Monsieur," or "Bonsoir" if it is nighttime.

OBTAINING CASH

Use your ATM card to obtain euros. The exchange rate is much better when you deal directly with your bank, rather than the hotels or the "Exchange" business on the street.

NEW BICYCLE PROGRAM IN PARIS

While we are about *PowerHiking* and the metro is very easy to use, there is a new program of bicycle rentals as of July 2007. The program is called VELIB'— a combination of "vélo" for bike and "liberté" for liberty. It is a very exciting program as one can still get exercise while combining *PowerHikes* to fit more fun into one day. VELIB' is flexible because you pick up a bike in one location and drop it off at another. There are stations all over town and you can buy a one-day pass, a seven-day pass, or a year pass and credit cards are accepted! You do need to provide your own helmet and need to familiarize yourself with bicycle rules in Paris. Each station has vending machines in eight languages. Put in your credit card, select your bike, push a button, and pull the bike out of the stand. Each bike has a basket and a lock. When you return it, slide the bike into the stand until you hear a beep and see a blinking light. For more information on this new program, go to www.velib.paris.fr.

THE RIVER SEINE

PowerHiking the Seine is one of the truly lovely adventures in Paris. On Sundays the quays on either side of the Seine are open to walkers from the Bastille to the Tour Eiffel and closed to cars. Watch out, however, for the skaters and bikers.

PowerHiking PARIS

is dedicated to John and Rodney

CONTENTS

CHAPTER 1

LES CHAMPS-ÉLYSÉES

DISTANCE 10.5 MILES | **TIME** 8 HOURS

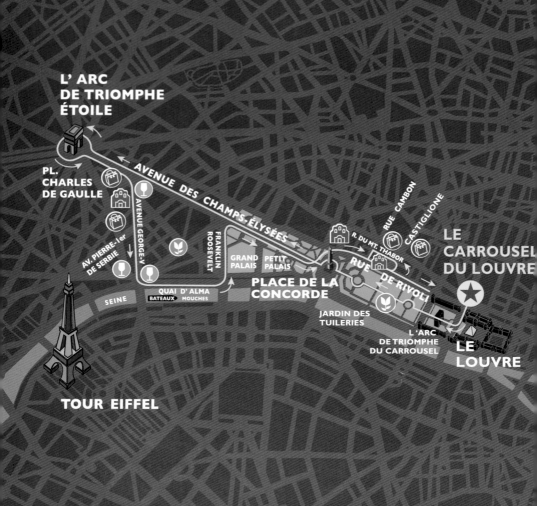

Paris is an exciting city, full of history.

You will want to see the most famous

sites first, and we lead you to the

Triumphal Way—through the Jardin des

Tuileries, to the place de la Concorde,

and up the avenue des Champs-Élysées to

L' Arc de Triomphe. **We start our** *PowerHike* today from the automobile

throughway just past the

Carrousel entrance to the

Louvre on the rue de Rivoli.

From your hotel, head towards

the Louvre.

Pass through the arched roadway and into the courtyard in the center of the Louvre adjacent to the glass pyramid. We do not go into the Louvre today, but stay in the fresh air and walk towards l'Arc de Triomphe

du Petit Carrousel, built in celebration of Napoleon's victories. As you pass by, you enter the Jardin des Tuileries. Situated next to the Seine, the Jardin des Tuileries is an example of Parisian life at its best and a good example of formal French gardens. Walk through the garden

towards the place de la Concorde,

enjoying the flowers, trees, statuary,

and the Parisians. It is approximately

a 12-minute (one-half mile) walk

through the Tuileries. As you approach

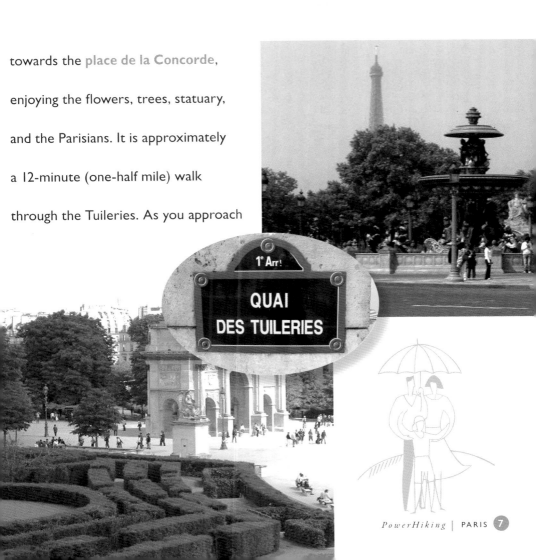

QUAI
DES TUILERIES

1ᵉ Arrᵗ

the gate to the place de la Concorde, you will see the Librairie des jardins aux Tuileries—a small bookstore dedicated to gardens. Have a look, but if you buy, be prepared to carry your purchase.

At the place de la Concorde, you will stand where Louis XVI and Marie Antoinette were beheaded and share in the history of the French Revolution. The column in the square is topped by an obelisk from the Egyptian Temple of Luxor. Circle around to the right and pass

the famous Hôtel du Crillon, the rue Gabriel, and the place de l'Alma. As you

pass through the park, you come

to the Triumphal Way, one of the

most famous avenues in the world:

Napoleon in victory, De Gaulle following

World War II, the Tour de France—the

Avenue des Champs-Élysées.

Tree-lined and beautiful, it is the center of action in Paris.

Continue walking up the slight incline of la grande avenue towards L'Arc de

Triomphe. You will pass Pavillon Élysées, the Restaurant Le Nôtre, and the

Presidential Palace. At avenue Winston Churchill, you will come to the Grand

Palais and the Petit Palais. Built for the World Exhibition in 1900, they house

art exhibits and you may want to take time to visit them.

At Rond Point des Champs-Élysées we begin to see the many shops and sidewalk cafés. Enjoy the fountains, flowers, and trees, and people-watch as you make your way to L' Arc de Triomphe. Cross place De Gaulle and, if you wish,

go to the top of the monument for your first views of the city. At this point you have *PowerHiked* over an hour and between 2½ to 3 miles.

For those with less time or who wish a shorter walk, become a part of Paris life at one of the many sidewalk cafés, or you may wish to return to your hotel. It is a pleasant walk or a short taxi or metro ride.

If you wish to see more, cross la grande avenue and head back down the Champs-Élysées on the other side, turning right on avenue George V (Fouquet's Brasserie—one of the most famous in Paris and worth a stop for refreshment—is on one corner and Louis Vuitton is on the other).

You are now on the avenue George V heading towards the Seine and your first sighting of the Tour Eiffel. Avenue George V is a very upscale street with high fashion houses, such as Dior and Zegna, and the famous Hotel George V. You will also pass the renowned gourmet shop, Hédiard, on the corner of avenue George V and avenue Pierre 1er de Serbie. Wander inside for a special treat—

chocolate, fruit candies, ice cream, or pastry. You can even purchase a meal and bottle of wine to go.

Continue your *PowerHike* toward the river and the quai d'Alma. On one corner is the Café George V and on the other is the Café Francis—both

perfect spots for a refreshment break and for enjoying the view of the Tour Eiffel.

Cross the busy quayside boulevard at the place de l' Alma to the Bateaux Mouches. We suggest the

Bateaux Mouches (relaxing riverboats) for an informative, narrated, one-hour trip on the Seine, viewing many famous landmarks such as Notre-Dame Cathedral, the Musée D'Orsay, and the Tour Eiffel along the way. Following your cruise, you may choose to walk to the Tour Eiffel, the place du Trocadero and the Palais Chaillot, or return by taxi or metro to

Toiles marouflées originales et soieries inspirent plénitude du repos et félicité du séjour.

Original hacked pictures and silks inspire an abundance of peace and a blissful stay

your hotel. For the strong of heart and leg, retrace your steps to the Champs-Élysées and the Jardin des Tuileries, or stay outside of the gardens on the rue du Rivoli. There is an interesting English bookstore on the corner of rue de Rivoli and rue Cambon. Remember, you must carry what you purchase, but you are nearing the end of the journey.

Turn down rue Cambon to find fancy lingerie shops, or continue on rue de Rivoli to rue Castiglione and the beautiful patio bar at the Westin Hotel. You have earned a well-deserved refreshment and can relax and think about shopping for perfume at Catherine a block away or fragrant soaps from Annick Goutal across the street. Begin to think about dinner, either at Le Soufflé around the corner

on **rue Mont Thabor** or at one of the many cafés along the stroll back to your hotel. Across the street from the Westin is a highly regarded Parisian restaurant, **Carré des Feuillants**, which used to be a cloistered convent.

It is time to go back to your hotel and a much-deserved rest. For those who chose a shorter version of this *PowerHike*, add in the segments of this walk that you missed to one of your other days. Remember your favorite sights so that you can return on another day.

CHAPTER 2

THE LOUVRE AND THE LEFT BANK

DISTANCE 10 MILES | **TIME 7 HOURS**

LE CARROUSEL DU LOUVRE

JARDIN DES TUILERIES

SEINE

LE LOUVRE

PONT ROYAL

RUE DE RIVOLI

R. DES ST. PÈRES

RUE JACOB

ST. GERMAIN DES PRÉS

BOUL. ST. GERMAIN

PALAIS DE JUSTICE

STE. CHAPELLE

RUE LUTECE

QUAI AUX FLEURS

RUE DE LA CITÉ

PONT AU DOUBLE

RUE DE LA HUCHETTE

RUE DE LA HARPE

NOTRE DAME

PONT ST. LOUIS

PONT MARIE

RUE DE L'ODÉON

ODÉON

BOUL. ST. MICHEL

CLUNY

PONT DE L'ARCHEVECHE

ILE ST. LOUIS

JARDIN DU LUXEMBOURG

The Louvre opens at 9 AM (closed on Tuesday) and is a logical first destination for today's *PowerHike*. You will arrive before the tour buses. We start at the Carrousel entrance, the easiest location to purchase entrance tickets. There are machines inside that take credit cards and you will avoid the long lines at the Pyramid entrance (designed by famed architect I. M. Pei). If you plan to spend the entire day in the museum enjoying its incredible grandeur, plan a leisurely lunch at the Café Marly on the

Louvre terrace overlooking the Pyramid and the grande esplanade. Today will be your day to tour the legendary collections and you can visit the Left Bank another day.

Entering the Louvre through the Carrousel entrance you pass through the Carrousel du Louvre Mall. This mall is a shopper's delight and you should take time to peruse the shops sometime during your visit. At this point you need to make some choices as to what you want to see first in the museum. Plan about two hours for your visit today so you have plenty of time to *PowerHike* the Left Bank.

After your visit, exit the Louvre through the Pyramid and emerge into the Jardin des Tuileries. Cross over the Seine on the Pont Royal and

take rue des Saints Pères into the St. Germain des Prés neighborhood.

St. Germain was once home to artists, writers, and intellectuals such as Hemingway, Sartre, Balzac, and Oscar Wilde. Rue des Saints Pères is a charming street with furniture makers, antique shops, and art galleries. Turn left onto rue de l'Université which becomes rue Jacob. Rue Jacob is a good example of today's Left Bank, a neighborhood of boutiques, galleries, and fashion. Turn right at rue de l'Échaud and you will be in front of one of the oldest churches in Paris, l'Église St. Germain. Step inside to get the feel of history in a still-functioning community place of worship. Immediately across from the church, at the corner of place Saint Germain des

Prés, is the iconic literary landmark, Café des Deux Magots, the meeting place of great writers of the 20th century such as Sartre and Hemingway. Enjoy lunch under

the umbrellas before continuing your journey.

Your *PowerHike* of the Left Bank continues by turning left down the **boulevard St. Germain** to **rue de l' Odéon**, passing around one of the oldest active theaters in Paris, **l'Odéon Théâtre de l'Europe** to the **Palais du Luxembourg**. The Palais du Luxembourg,

at the entrance to the Jardin du Luxembourg,

was the home of Catherine de Medici and today

houses the French Senate. Experience the serenity

of the garden as you wander through the beautiful

fountains and planted flower beds, or relax at one

of the cafes just outside the garden. As you emerge

on **boulevard**

St. Michel, turn left and

follow the boulevard towards

the **Seine**,

stopping

to gaze at

the ancient

site of the founding of Paris,

the **l'Abbaye de Cluny**. Just

across from Cluny on the right

is a small alley named rue de la

Harpe. Follow it towards the

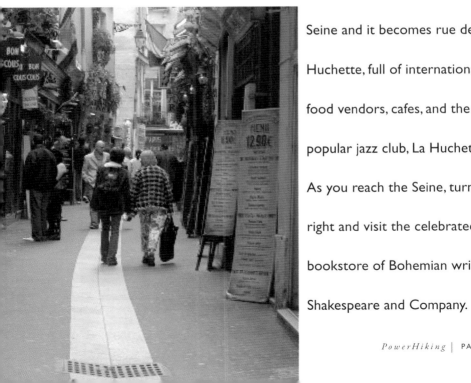

Seine and it becomes rue de la Huchette, full of international food vendors, cafes, and the popular jazz club, La Huchette. As you reach the Seine, turn right and visit the celebrated bookstore of Bohemian writers, Shakespeare and Company.

Cross the Seine on **Pont au Double** to **Notre-Dame Cathedral**. Notre-Dame is impressive for its size, the flying buttresses and gothic arched ceiling, the beauty of the interior, and stained glass windows. It houses the largest pipe organ in France. Visit the inside (lines may be long but move quickly) and also visit the towers for beautiful views of the Seine and Paris. Leave Notre-Dame and turn right on **rue de la Cité**, then left on **rue Lutèce** where you will pass the flower market and, just past the **Palais de Justice**, visit **Sainte-Chapelle**. Built in the 13th century, **Sainte-Chapelle** houses some of the most beautiful stained glass windows in Paris. Continue up the **quai aux Fleurs** and

cross over the bridge to the picturesque **Île St. Louis** and **Berthillon**, famous for ice cream and the view back to Notre-Dame. Criss-cross the narrow streets of Île St. Louis and take in the charm of its small boutiques, cafes and

galleries. Cross back over the Seine to the Right Bank at the Pont Marie and continue straight ahead to the **rue de Rivoli**. Turn left and head back to the Louvre and your hotel.

CHAPTER 3

MUSÉE D'ORSAY
HÔTEL DES INVALIDES
MUSÉE RODIN

DISTANCE 12 MILES **TIME** 8 HOURS

LE MUSÉE D'ORSAY

LES INVALIDES

LE TOMBEAU DE NAPOLÉON

LE MUSÉE DE RODIN

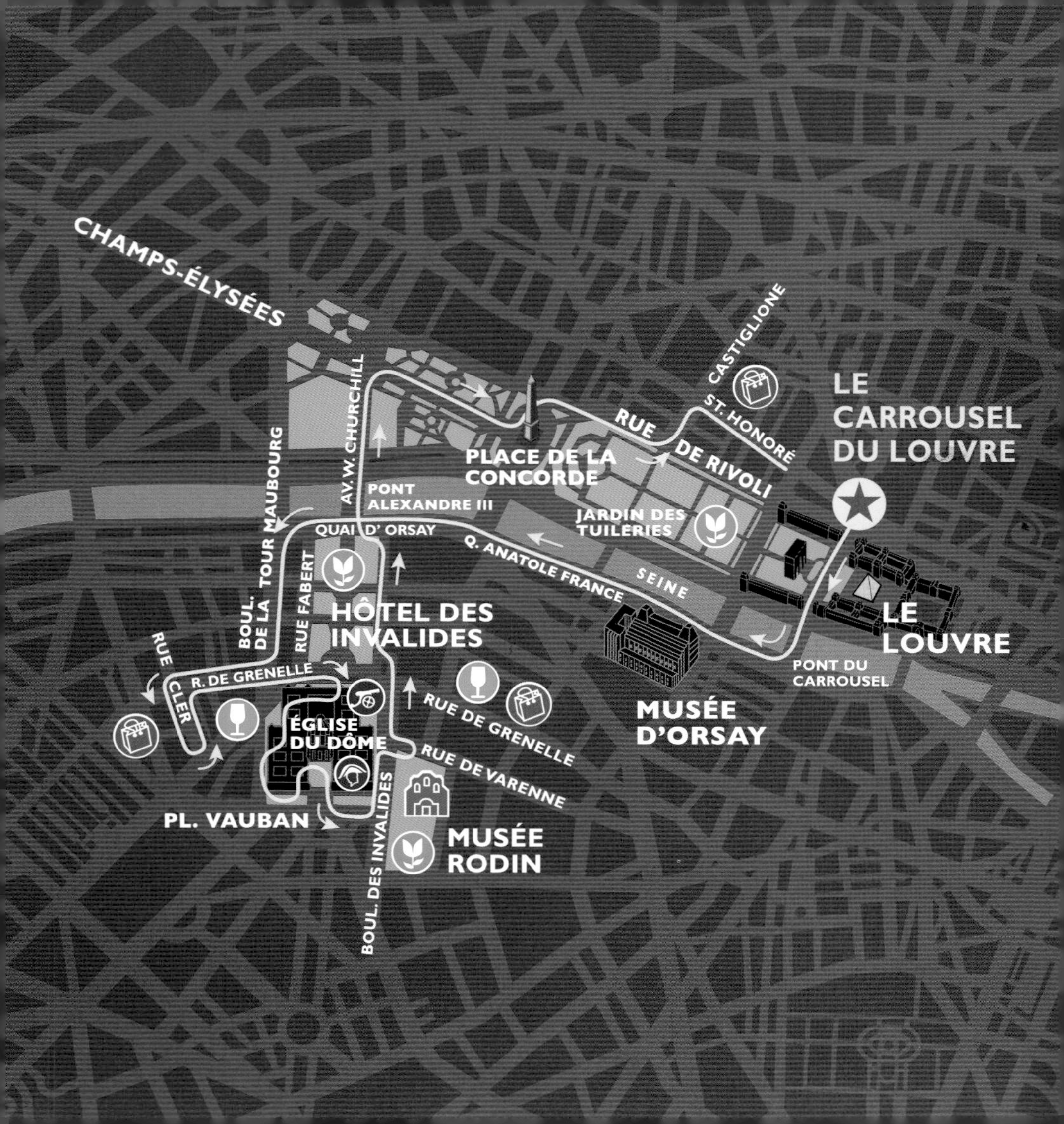

CHAMPS-ÉLYSÉES
AV. W. CHURCHILL
CASTIGLIONE
LE CARROUSEL DU LOUVRE
RUE DE RIVOLI
ST. HONORÉ
PLACE DE LA CONCORDE
BOUL. DE LA TOUR MAUBOURG
PONT ALEXANDRE III
JARDIN DES TUILERIES
QUAI D' ORSAY
Q. ANATOLE FRANCE
SEINE
RUE FABERT
HÔTEL DES INVALIDES
LE LOUVRE
RUE CLER
R. DE GRENELLE
PONT DU CARROUSEL
RUE DE GRENELLE
MUSÉE D'ORSAY
ÉGLISE DU DÔME
RUE DE VARENNE
PL. VAUBAN
BOUL. DES INVALIDES
MUSÉE RODIN

Today is a feast of museums. You can visit all three museums and *PowerHike* 12.3 miles or you can decide to shorten the day and visit only one or two. Whatever your choice, it will be a memorable *PowerHike* through French culture. The Musée d'Orsay was originally a train station, built for the 1900 World's Fair, and now houses Impressionist paintings and French art from the second half of the 19th century. There are various contemporary exhibits, and the central area of the first floor houses a permanent

collection of statuary. It is a beautiful building with a huge domed roof—truly

a beautiful sight to behold as you walk into the museum. Because there is such

an extensive collection of paintings by Claude Monet, it is a good idea to visit

the Musée d'Orsay before you visit Giverny.

The *PowerHike* to the Musée d'Orsay is an

easy half mile from the Jardin des Tuileries

over the Pont du Carrousel and along the

quai Anatole France. Allow a couple of

hours for the museum, which adds enjoyable

miles to your *PowerHike*. Be sure to visit the two-story bookstore at the front

of the museum. Before continuing on to Les Invalides,

Église du Dôme

TOMBEAU
DE NAPOLÉON
Tomb of Napoleon

take in the local artists around the museum and the

quai.

It is three-fourths of a mile along the quai Anatole France to Hôtel des Invalides and the beautiful Esplanade des Invalides. As you *PowerHike* towards the Hôtel des Invalides, you can watch groups of Parisians picnicking and enjoying the beautiful grounds. Les Invalides has a rich military history, being a barracks, hospital, and now a military museum. The dome holds the tomb of Napoleon.

Moving away from the river on rue Fabert, you will pass rue de Grenelle on the right. For a quick diversion, turn right to rue Cler for some very chic shops, including many gourmet cheese and food shops. These shops would be

perfect for purchasing a picnic for the Esplanade

des Invalides. Retrace your steps to the

boulevard de la Tour Maubourg and the Café

de l'Esplanade. The café (with its cannonball light

fixtures and cannon on the wall) is a popular spot

for lunch. The food is special, as is

the view of Les Invalides. After lunch,

walk over to the Musée de l'Armée.

There are exhibits of weaponry,

uniforms, and memorabilia—a definite

must for the military buff. The bookstore is a good source for military books

and toy soldiers. Proceed to the place Vauban and enter the Tombeau de Napoléon. For those saving the Musée Rodin for another day, it is a short, mild *PowerHike* on to the Tour Eiffel and the Trocadéro, from which you can follow the river back to the Tuileries and your hotel.

From le Tombeau de Napoléon, turn left on boulevard des Invalides to rue de Varenne and the Musée Rodin. This museum is a visual treat and one of the loveliest in Paris. Wander through the house where Rodin lived and

worked, and then stroll the gardens full of roses and sculptures, such as **The Gates of Hell** and **The Thinker**. Notice the view of the Tour Eiffel from the garden. There are several cafes nearby and a quick refreshment or a bottle of

water is a good idea before the *PowerHike* back to the hotel.

Leaving the Musée Rodin you can turn right on rue de Varenne, left on rue de Bourgogne and right on rue de Grennelle and visit some of the chic neighborhood shops, or you can turn left on rue de Varenne and cross to boulevard des Invalides and follow it towards the river, crossing the Seine on the **Pont Alexandre III**. One of the most beautiful bridges crossing the

Seine, it was built for the World Exhibition in 1900. Proceed to the Champs-

Élysées and turn right following the beautiful plane trees to the place de la

Concorde and the rue de Rivoli. At rue Castiglione, turn left and walk to

the corner of rue St. Honoré. You will find Annick Goutal, famous for soaps,

perfumes, and creams. Indulge and shop or relax and visit their spa.

Today you *PowerHiked* 12.3 miles, and

- Got a refresher course on Monet and the Impressionists

- Became acquainted with France's military heroes

- Wandered through beautiful gardens

- Learned about France's most famous sculptor, Rodin

- Shopped in special boutiques

CHAPTER 4

LE MARAIS

DISTANCE 5 MILES | **TIME 3-4** HOURS

LE CARROUSEL DU LOUVRE

LE LOUVRE

SEINE

RUE DE RIVOLI

RUE DE RIVOLI

RUE DU TEMPLE

ARCHIVES NATIONALES

MUSÉE CARNAVALET HISTOIRE DE PARIS

MUSÉE PICASSO

RUE DES FRANCS BOURGEOIS

HÔTEL DE SULLY

HÔTEL DE VILLE

VILLAGE ST. PAUL

RUE ST. ANTOINE

PLACE DES VOSGES

SEINE

Le Marais is an old Jewish neighborhood now filled wih people of all faiths, cultures, and socio-economic backgrounds.

It is a vibrant residential community where small merchants still exist to serve their neighbors. There

is every kind of food store, hardware store, cleaners, clothing store, and pharmacy. The streets are full of people going about running a household or a business.

Another layer to this neighborhood is the

presence of some very old, ornate buildings called *hôtels particuliers*. These

were the grand

residences of former

high government

officials and nobles

during the monarchy, now used mostly as museums. They are very interesting

to visit, and if you can manage to see one or two of them during your

adventure to the Marais, the better

known is the Musée Picasso. There

is also the Musée Carnavalet

Histoire de Paris. A very recent

addition to the neighborhood is

a number of trendy boutiques

—designer clothes, shoe stores,

a knitting boutique and an

irresistible chocolate shop. On

the edge of all of this activity and vibrance is a rabbit warren of antique stores

called the **Village St. Paul**. The Marais

is a richly stimulating neighborhood,

perfect for a *PowerHike*.

Take our main

PowerHiking

artery, the rue

de Rivoli, to the **Hôtel de Ville** and turn up to the

left, away from the Seine, to the **rue du Temple**. You will pass the **Archives**

Nationales and *Musée Carnavalet*

Histoire de Paris. Directions to the

Musée Picasso are well marked here

as well.

The best trendy street is **rue des Francs Bourgeois**. Turn right off rue du Temple

and follow this chic street all the way to the **place des Vosges**. This is one of the most elegant small parks in Paris, surrounded by the perfectly symmetrical, classic French buildings that were once aristocratic homes and government offices. Today they house mostly government

offices. The surrounding area is a very desirable

location for Parisians to live. There are also many cafés and shops. The impressive *hôtel particulier*, Hôtel de Sully, is on the corner towards the Seine. Just across the rue St. Antoine is l'Église St. Paul and, behind it, the antique shops of Village St. Paul. Return to your hotel on the

rue de Rivoli.

NOTE: The French translation of "window shopping" is "window licking" or *lèche-vitrines*. This **PowerHike** provides you with lots of windows to lick!

CHAPTER 5

FAUBOURG ST. HONORÉ

DISTANCE 4.5 MILES | TIME ALL DAY

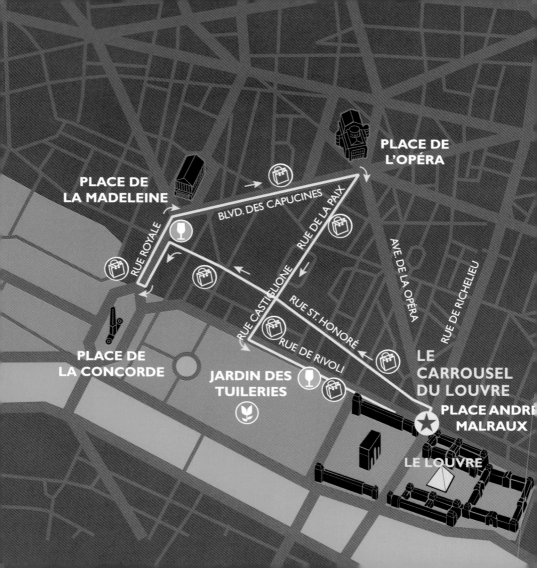

The words Paris and fashion are synonymous and a trip to Paris is not complete without a trip down rue Faubourg St. Honoré, home to the top fashion houses of the world. But *PowerHiking* and fashion? *PowerHiking* and the rue Faubourg St. Honoré? Yes! This is Power Shopping! Put on your special outfit and don your fancy *PowerHiking* shoes.

We begin at the Carrousel entrance of the Louvre and proceed to place André Malraux and turn left on rue St. Honoré. There is a myriad of clothing,

crystal, porcelain, and jewelry shops and you will want to shop both sides of the street so as not to miss a single boutique or a single beautiful item. While rue St. Honoré has shops of every description, it is rue Faubourg St. Honoré that is home to top European designers. Towards the end of rue

Faubourg St. Honoré you will

pass the **American Embassy**

and a little further on the Élysées

Palace, home to the president

of France. Your ultimate goal is

Hermès on rue du Faubourg St. Honoré. On the way you will pass **Hervé**

Chapelier (tote bags in wonderful bright colors), **Etro**, **Ferragamo**,

Versace, **Escada**, **Gucci**, **Laura Ashley**, **Laurel**, **Max Mara**, **Roberto**

Cavalli, Tod's, Zapa, Façonnable, Lacoste, Lanvin, Sonia Rykiel, Yves Saint Laurent, Longchamp, Cristal Lalique, Elma Miro, and many other boutiques and cafes, including Bernardaud Salon de Thé. At rue Castiglione, visit Annick Goutal for delightful-smelling soaps and lotions. A little further down on the other side of the street is Catherine, a shop for all of your makeup and perfume needs. Catherine also has wonderful knockoff handbags and will ship everything home that you cannot carry. Rue Castiglione is also home to Cristal Vendôme, a tantalizingly beautiful store with shelves

full of **Baccarat**, **Lladro**, **Lalique**, and other

irresistible pieces—and they ship! Retrace your

steps back to rue St. Honoré. Around the corner

from the Westin Hotel you will pass Hôtel

Costes, a very trendy French hotel with avant-

garde décor and a hot local bar scene. After

visiting this trendy spot, continue shopping on your way to rue Royale.

At the corner of rue St. Honoré and rue Royale turn right and take a much-deserved break (shopping can be exhausting!) and visit Ladurée, a celebrated French tea room, for lunch, tea, or a fabulous dessert. After your refreshment, turn left on rue Royale, as you leave Ladurée, and walk the block to rue de Rivoli. Cross rue Royale and return down the other side of the street. Across the street from Ladurée is a charming alley with a delightful outdoor café and boutiques, such as Anne Fontaine, which are too wonderful to resist. If you are fond of Anne Fontaine, be sure to visit Rayeure on our *PowerHike* of the Marais.

Continue shopping on rue Royale in the direction of La Madeleine. La Madeleine is a famous Parisian church, almost turned into a temple to the Grand

Army by Napoleon. Wander in to visit and, as you come out, you will pass

Hédiard and Maille on the left and Fauchon on the right. At Hédiard you can

purchase fruit candies (for which they are famous), chocolate, and other gourmet

items. At Maille there is an array

of different flavored mustards and

seasonings. Well-known Fauchon

is equally appealing for chocolates and gourmet items. Follow the plaza around

to the right to boulevard Capucines and walk in the direction of l'Opéra,

passing many wonderful shops

including François Pinet and Baccarat.

At rue de la Paix you have a choice.

Continue in the direction of l'Opéra

and stop at the Café Opéra,

a Parisian favorite. You can

also visit inside l'Opéra, a

grand Parisian building with a

magnificent staircase and foyer.

Your other choice is to turn right at

rue de la Paix and

follow it to **place**

Vendôme. Place

Vendôme is not only beautiful, but famous—home to the **Hôtel Ritz**, **Hôtel Vendôme**, **Bucherer**, **Dior**, and other designer shops. On the other side of place Vendôme, rue de la Paix becomes rue Castiglione (remember Annick Goutal and Catherine!). Continue down rue Castiglione to rue de Rivoli and turn left. Rue de Rivoli is home to many shops of crystal, clothing, and items to remember Paris with, as well as cafés and ice cream shops. You cannot miss a visit to **Angelina**, a Parisian favorite for ice cream, chocolates, pastry, and the richest, creamiest French hot chocolate. They also have beautiful boxes of chocolates to purchase. Angelina is a special spot to end your *PowerHike* and you are quite near the Carrousel, where you began the day.

CHAPTER 6

BOIS DE BOULOGNE
LE PARC DE BAGATELLE

DISTANCE 5+ MILES | **TIME** 5 HOURS

LE MUSÉE MARMOTTAN

....

LE BOIS DE BOULOGNE
LAC SUPÉRIEUR • LAC INFÉRIEUR

....

LE PARC DE BAGATELLE

....

ROSE GARDEN

....

L'ORANGERIE

....

CHÂTEAU DE BAGATELLE

....

L'HIPPODROME DE LONGCHAMP

....

ROLAND GARROS TENNIS COMPLEX

....

RUE DU PASSY

....

68

CHÂTEAU
DE BAGATELLE

BOIS
DE
BOULOGNE

ALLÉE DU BORD DE L'EAU

BELVEDERE

L'ORANGERIE

ALLÉE DE LONGCHAMP

LAC
INFÉRIEUR

LA MUETTE

AVE. DE L'HIPPODROME

BLVD. SUCHET

MUSÉE
MARMOTTAN

LAC
SUPÉRIEUR

This huge open-space parkland, which is the Bois de Boulogne, was once the hunting grounds of the kings of France. There are two lakes, Lac Supérieur, which is about ⅔ of a mile around, and Lac Inférieur, about 1½ miles around. Both have paths around them. You can also rent boats on Lac Inférieur and row around the island in the middle. On the island is the Châlet des Îles, a restaurant in a beautiful setting with wonderful views. There is also a ferry boat to the island. The Bois is a bit far from the center of Paris so you need to take the metro to La Muette. Exit at "La Muette" and walk up avenue Ingres to route des Lacs à Passy. Cross boulevard Suchet and avenue du Maréchal Franchet d'Espérey, where there is a passage over the beltway, to the Bois. The Musée Marmottan, with its Monet collection, is worth a quick detour. Turn right on boulevard Suchet to rue Louis-Boilly and the *musée*. It is open everyday except Mondays. After seeing the *musée*, turn left on boulevard

Suchet and continue back to route des Lacs à Passy. Turn right to the Bois. Following your lake adventure, *PowerHike* back in the direction that you came from and return to the "La Muette" metro station. This is not an area for an evening *PowerHike*—daytime only.

DISTANCE 4 MILES | **TIME** 3 HOURS

A very special destination in a different section of the Bois de Boulogne is the **Parc de Bagatelle**. The spectacular rose garden is not to

be missed. Take the metro to "Neuilly" and bus #43 along route de Sèvres à Neuilly to the entrance to Bagatelle. Stroll among the hundreds of rose varieties and be amazed by the unusual and stunning colors. It is a vast collection of very old varietals, as well as new ones. The layout and plant design of the garden are breathtaking and inspiring. This is truly a feast for the senses. Take photos to guide you with your

future rose garden plans! The garden is seasonal—bulbs in the spring, roses at their best in June. There is also an incredible wall of iris. Behind the rose garden is another impressive flower and herb garden. **L'Orangerie**, site of many summer night concerts, is a building of beautiful, classical architecture,

used for raising orange trees in the winter. Parisians come with delicious picnics to enjoy concerts in the rose garden. After you have wandered through the gardens, take the winding path, bordered by hedges, up to the "belvedere" and gaze out over

the Bois de Boulogne and the city beyond. This is one of the most special overlooks in Paris. Walk back down and follow the path along the sprawling lawns, where couples lounge and artists sketch, continuing past the resident flock of peacocks to the classically

designed small chateau, le Château de Bagatelle. Bagatelle means trifle and the chateau was commissioned to be built in 1777 by Marie Antoinette. It now

houses ever-changing art exhibits throughout the year, such as silk tapestries, and

porcelain from Sèvres. On your way back to the entrance to the *parc*, stop at

the leafy café for a leisurely lunch.

DISTANCE 1 ½ MILES | **TIME** 2 HOURS

A short walk from Le Parc de Bagatelle is the **Hippodrome de Longchamp**,

site of French horseracing. For another adventure, follow rue Michel-Ange to

rue d' Auteuil and continue your *PowerHike* on the grounds of Roland Garros,

home of the French Open Tennis Tournament, held in early June. You can

also continue on to rue du Passy for some pricey shopping in the toney 16th

arrondissement.

JARDIN BOTANIQUE
DE LA VILLE DE PARIS
BAGATELLE

Parc
de
Bagatelle

CHAPTER 7

MONTMARTRE SACRÉ-COEUR

DISTANCE 10 MILES **TIME 5** HOURS

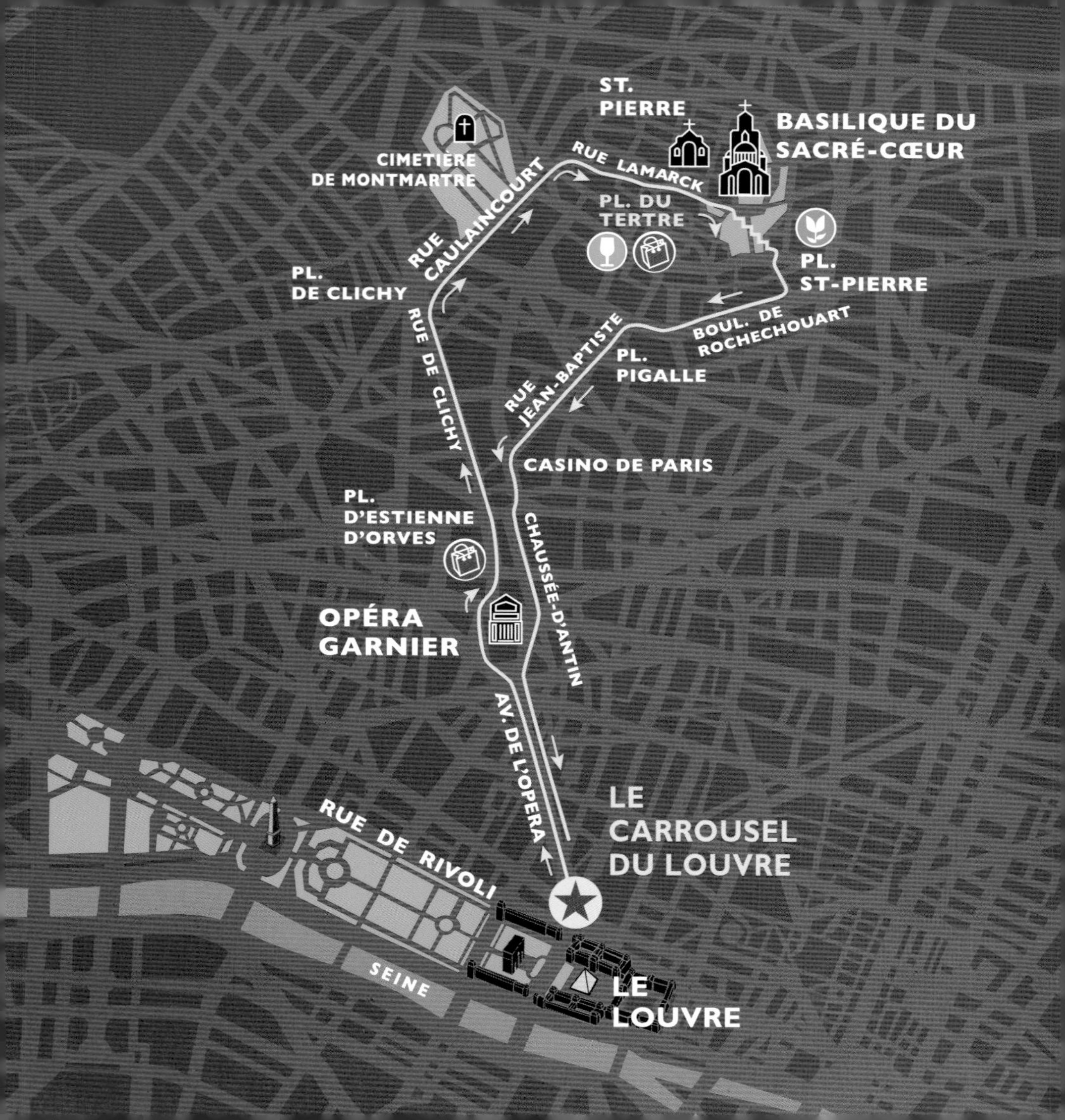
ST. PIERRE
BASILIQUE DU SACRÉ-CŒUR
CIMETIÈRE DE MONTMARTRE
RUE LAMARCK
PL. DU TERTRE
RUE CAULAINCOURT
PL. ST-PIERRE
PL. DE CLICHY
BOUL. DE ROCHECHOUART
RUE JEAN-BAPTISTE
PL. PIGALLE
RUE DE CLICHY
CASINO DE PARIS
PL. D'ESTIENNE D'ORVES
CHAUSSÉE-D'ANTIN
OPÉRA GARNIER
AV. DE L'OPERA
LE CARROUSEL DU LOUVRE
RUE DE RIVOLI
SEINE
LE LOUVRE

Artists, writers, eccentrics—

Montmartre is home to all. This

avant-garde area of Paris was home

to struggling 19th and 20th century

artists who shared stories and pastis

in smoky bars before moving on to

paint in the bright light of Provence.

Today the square is still filled with

artists painting local scenes and

portraits of passing tourists.

The *PowerHike* up to Montmartre

and Sacré-Coeur—the world famous basilica synonymous with Montmartre—

is difficult and steep. It is at least an hour up and an hour down, but well worth it for getting the flavor of the neighborhoods, which include both the glamorous and the gritty. From our starting point at the Carrousel du Louvre on rue de Rivoli, take avenue de l'Opéra to place de l'Opéra. Behind l'Opéra and the Galeries Lafayette department store, take rue de Clichy to place de

Clichy and turn right on rue Gaulaincourt, which borders the Cimetière Montmartre. Take time to visit the cimetière, as you will find the graves of many notable artists, such as Dégas, Zola, and Truffaut. Angle

to the right and uphill
into little streets such
as rue Lepic and rue
Gabrielle. You are
in Montmartre! You
will pass the original
Moulin Rouge and the
former homes of Van
Gogh, Picasso, Toulouse-
Lautrec, as well as
familiar scenes painted
by Renoir. Continue

up the hill to Sacré-Coeur. Visit inside the basilica and be mesmerized by the

panoramic view of Paris below. Visit **L'Église St. Pierre de Montmartre**, one

of the oldest church and graveyards in Paris, adjacent to Sacré-Coeur. On **rue

Lamark**, just to the right

world famous funicular

Follow rue Lamark to the

one of the many enticing

of the lookout point, is the

and tree-lined staircase.

place du Tertre and stop at

cafés, ice cream, or crêpe

stands. There are various local artisan shops to wander through and, of course,

fascinating artists to watch as they work. Retrace your steps to the staircase

and begin your *PowerHike* downhill, through ordinary Parisian neighborhoods,

eventually ending up at l'Opéra. Linger at the famous Café de l'Opéra for a

break and people watching.
If time permits, tour the inside
of l'Opéra.
To *PowerHike* up to
Montmartre and back is a
10-mile day. You can take
the metro or a taxi in one
direction in order to have more
time exploring the cemetery,
cathedral, shops, restaurants,
and iconic cabarets tucked away in
side streets.

CHAPTER 8

GIVERNY

VERNON

. . . .

GIVERNY

. . . .

MONET'S HOME

. . . .

MONET'S GARDEN

. . . .

AMERICAN ART MUSEUM
AND GARDENS

. . . .

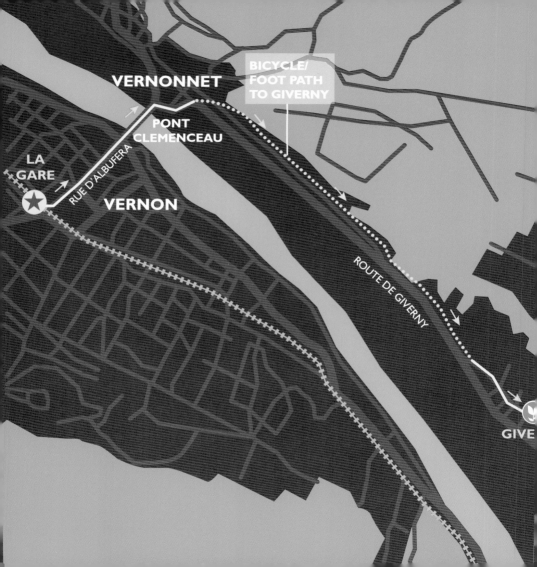

After seeing the Monet and other Impressionist paintings in the Musée d'Orsay,

you can now visit Claude Monet's home and garden in the timeless village of

Giverny, located about an hour outside Paris. Giverny was home to Monet

for over forty years and where he painted some of his most famous works, including the Water Lilies. Many of Monet's paintings were inspired by this

riverside village, his lily pond and glorious, multi-hued garden. The natural

beauty of Giverny and its environs inspired not only Monet, but many other

Impressionist artists who spent time there. Visit Monet's home, and the garden, as well as the American Art Museum. Afterwards, you can enjoy one of the cafés, then browse the shops and galleries. Giverny is a

perfect setting for a *PowerHike*.

We start at the Gare St. Lazare. If your hotel is close enough to walk, start your

PowerHike early. Otherwise, take a bicycle or taxi to the Gare St. Lazare and purchase a round-trip ticket on the Grand Ligne train to Vernon. Once you arrive in Vernon, you have some choices: take the 5-minute bus ride to Giverny; walk (about 3 miles, very easy and picturesque); or ride a bicycle (available at the café across from the train station). This is a *PowerHike*, so we walk! You will see many local residents on the well-marked path with their children and dogs.

From the train station, follow the main street through the village, pass the bakery, and cross over the bridge. Bring some water with you, available at the café across the street

from the station. Once over the bridge, follow the

brown road signs directing you to the path to Giverny.

The path is well designed for walkers and bicyclists,

and provides stunning views of the Seine and beyond, with glimpses into colorful

homes and gardens along the way. You will pass the local church and cemetery

where Monet is buried. Take a minute to visit.

At Giverny you have choices for lunch, but we

recommend Les Nymphéas (which also has a

"to go" window). You will not only love the food,

but also the pots of flowers and garden as well.

The shops are worth perusing because Giverny

is especially nice for gifts such as seeds for do-

it-yourself Monet plantings, Impressionist-inspired rain umbrellas, scarves, ties,

tableware, note paper, and art books. Enter the

Monet Foundation and walk into the awe-

inspiring garden. The garden is in two parts,

connected by an underground walkway. The

Clos Normand is the flower garden and The Water Garden is a pond Monet

created from the river  Epte. The Water

Garden is where you will see the lily

pond, the bridge, and Monet's boat, all

made famous in his paintings. Monet

enjoyed his garden in all seasons, but it is

at its best when the roses bloom. Visit the home where he lived and worked for

43 years, and where he entertained other famous painters and literary artists. It is mostly as it was when he resided there. As you leave, spend some time in the gift shop located in one of the studios he used for painting. Do not miss the ice cream cart located just outside.

After visiting the Monet home and garden, stroll over to the American Art Museum and gardens—more contemporary, but thoroughly pleasing. The gardens are organized by color. American artists came to Giverny to benefit from the unique quality of light that inspired the Impressionist school of painting.

Did you know that Americans contributed greatly to the

restoration of Monet's home

and garden?

When you have nearly

exhausted yourself in this

mecca of art and beauty, follow

the path back to Vernon to the

train station and the train back

to Paris. You can also choose

to follow the path to the

parking lot at Giverny and the

waiting bus back to Vernon and the train station.

CHAPTER 9

VERSAILLES

DISTANCE 10+ MILES | TIME 10 HOURS

LE CHÂTEAU DE VERSAILLES
THE COACH MUSEUM
THE KING'S APARTMENTS
THE HALL OF MIRRORS
THE QUEEN'S SUITE
THE CORONATION ROOM
THE CHAPEL ROYAL

....

LES JARDINS DE VERSAILLES
LE GRAND CANAL
L'ALLÉE ROYALE
APOLLO BASIN
COLLONADE GROVE

....

LE GRAND TRIANON

....

LE PETIT TRIANON

....

QUEEN'S THEATRE

....

QUEEN'S HAMLET

....

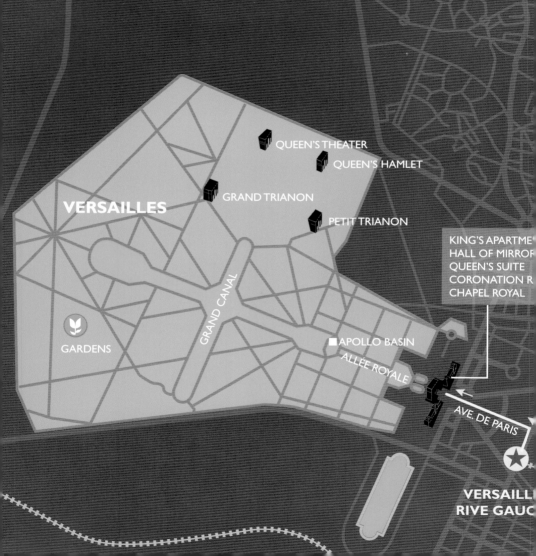

VERSAILLES

QUEEN'S THEATER

QUEEN'S HAMLET

GRAND TRIANON

PETIT TRIANON

KING'S APARTME
HALL OF MIRROR
QUEEN'S SUITE
CORONATION R
CHAPEL ROYAL

GRAND CANAL

■ APOLLO BASIN

GARDENS

ALLÉE ROYALE

AVE. DE PARIS

VERSAILL
RIVE GAUC

"To all the glories of France"

Versailles was originally a country hunting lodge of Louis XIII. Louis XIV (the Sun King) converted the lodge into a chateau second to none—a statement of grandeur, power, and beauty and an impressive monument to himself. Versailles is magnificent and you enter into its glorious history as soon as you walk through the gilded gates.

To visit Versailles, *PowerHike* to the train station at the Musée d'Orsay

—passing through the Jardin des Tuileries and across the

Seine. Purchase a ticket that includes the tours at the chateau

to avoid the long ticket lines upon arrival.

You will arrive at Versailles with a short walk to the chateau. Save your

exploration of the town for later. There are many areas

to visit at Versailles—the Coach Museum, the King's

Apartments, the Hall of Mirrors, the Queen's

Suite, the Coronation Room, the private apartments,

and the **Royal Chapel**. You will want to visit them all. Be sure to purchase an audio tour guide as you explore the halls of royalty. There are several bookstores inside, worth visiting for photographic guides and for books to lead you further into French history.

While you will *PowerHike* several miles through the chateau, the **gardens of Versailles** also beckon. They are gorgeous and extensive, including flowers, fountains, sculpture, and the **Grand**

Canal. *PowerHike* the Allée Royale,

venturing off to each side to see the Apollo

Basin, the various grottos, the beautifully

manicured flower beds, and the fountains and

statues. It is truly awe-inspiring. There are avenues, groves, mazes, fountains,

the Collonade Grove, and endless inviting sights, walks, and exercise. You

could spend the day in the gardens alone and *PowerHike* 10 to 15 miles.

There are special days throughout the year when the gardens' history comes alive with a water and light show. Not only are the gardens perfect for *PowerHiking*, but you can also rent bicycles outside the chateau grounds, and row boats on the Grand Canal. There are several cafés and ice cream stands tucked away in the hedges and along the Grand Canal—a perfect spot for refreshment.

Marie

After leaving

the royal

grounds,

follow

the tree-

lined path to the right in the

direction of the **Grand Trianon**

(originally built as a private

space for the king), the **Petit**

Trianon (private residence of Marie

Antoinette), the **Queen's Theatre** (an

informal society where the Queen herself

ᵉᵗᵉ
Le Pavillon français
ANGE-JACQUES GABRIEL, architecte
1749-1750

Lieu de repos et de collation édifié pour Louis XV.
Marie-Antoinette utilisait ce pavillon pour ses fêtes,
ses bals et ses concerts, lui adjoignant alors une tente
démontable. Salon rond central à la corniche décorée
d'oiseaux, dorée au XIXᵉ siècle.

performed), and the Queen's Hamlet. The hamlet is modeled on a Normandy

village and was a working farm including fishing, dairy, cheese making, a water

mill, and vegetable gardens. A special project of Marie Antoinette, the hamlet

takes you into a uniquely rural environment separate from the grandeur of

the chateau.

Retrace your steps to the Grand Canal and return along the manicured paths and gardens to the chateau. After miles of *PowerHiking* it is still difficult to leave the glorious grounds behind. Ignore the many people hawking goods and continue back toward the

train station. If energy and time permit, now is the time to explore the town of Versailles or just relax on the train back to Paris. Cross back over the Seine and through the Jardin des Tuileries to your hotel. Today you have *PowerHiked* in the paths of kings and queens in "the glory that was France" before the French Revolution.

BERCY

Bercy is a newly reinvented neighborhood, located in the southeast corner of Paris. Once industrial and the center for commercial wine storage and wine trading, the smokestacks belched pollutants into the air, railroad tracks ran through the area, and no one went there for enjoyment. Today, however, industry has moved further outside of Paris, and the wine caves have been creatively converted into trendy cafés

with outside terraces and **cour St. Émilion**, the newest Parisian shopping mall. There is a unique bookstore/café/wine

store, **ALICE**, which is a must-see. Bercy is a perfect spot for lunch and also a very trendy, upscale location for cocktails. The newness and modernity of the

neighborhood is an intriguing contrast to the venerable streets of old Paris. Immediately adjacent to cour St. Émilion is **Parc de Bercy** – another urban renewal project and one of the grands *projets* of former

French President François Mitterrand. *PowerHike* past the lake, fountains, old wine train rails, and planted vineyards. Follow a bridge over the street towards

the playgrounds, beautiful trees, and paths that lead you to a massive staircase at the other side of the park. Walk up the stairs and—SURPRISE!—you are at the amazingly modern **Pont de Tolbiac** spanning the Seine. On the other side of the bridge, on the Quai de la Gare, is the **Bibliothèque Nationale de France–François Mitterrand**. Built in 1996, the huge national library is another one of Mitterrand's grands *projets*. The library is open to the public so you may explore inside or simply enjoy the view of the river and the nearby

Ministère des Finances from the amazing Pont de Tolbiac. You will see next to

quai de la Gare houseboats and the very trendy boat/nightclubs docked on the

river and frequented by the young professionals working and socializing in this

area now.

This is a perfect afternoon *PowerHike* if you plan to have lunch in a former

wine cave! From the Palais-Royal metro station take the #1 line in the direction of Nation, then transfer to the #6 line in the direction of Charles de Gaulle, exiting at Cour St. Émilion. Walk into the pedestrian mall and stroll along looking at menus until you find a free table. Enjoy the people watching and a fine French lunch! Afterwards browse through ALICE for some gift shopping. Then head to the Parc de Bercy and walk towards the massive staircase. Once you have enjoyed the other side of the Pont de Tolbiac, go back down the staircase and head to the north side of the *parc* and the Bercy stadium, the **Palais Omnisports de Paris-Bercy**, a 16,000-seat stadium for sporting events and concerts. Circle the stadium to the Bercy metro stop, and go back the way you came, this time taking the #6 line in the direction of Nation and transferring to the #1 line in the direction of La Défense, exiting at Palais-Royal.

CHAPTER 11

PARC DE MONCEAU

DISTANCE 3+ MILES　**TIME 3+** HOURS

PARC DE
MONCEAU

MUSÉE
CERNUSCHI

L' ARC
DE TRIOMPHE
ÉTOILE

AV. HOCHE

RUE DE MONCEAU

HÔTEL DE
CAMONDO

AVENUE VALASQUEZ

BOUL. MALESHERBES

AVENUE
VICTOR HUGO

PL. CHARLES
DE GAULLE

AVENUE DES CHAMPS-ÉLYSÉES

PL. VICTOR
HUGO

SEINE

Parc de Monceau is a charming neighborhood

park where you will see much Parisian life—

residents strolling, sitting and chatting on the

park benches, and you hear the exuberant

sound of children playing.

This is an upscale neighborhood—gated, with impressive homes and a private

school where the playground is this beautifully

manicured park. Walk through the gates to see

the variety of plantings, then pass through the

magnificent gate onto avenue Velasquez and

visit Musée Cernuschi, on the right, to view the

collection of Chinese art. Continue on avenue Velasquez to boulevard

Malesherbes, a chic neighborhood with inviting ethnic shops and cafes. Continue your *PowerHike* to the right on boulevard Malesherbes to rue de Monceau and the **Musée Nissim de Camondo**. The **Hôtel de Camondo** was the home of a wealthy Parisian banking family terribly affected by the events of World Wars I and II. The mansion is now a museum representing the lifestyle at the turn of the 20th century. Include the audio guide in your tour, as there is a narrated history of the mansion,

of each room, and of the extensive collection of 18th-century antiques. Linger as long as you wish in the mansion and then return on rue de Monceau to boulevard Malesherbes and the Parc de Monceau. While this has not been a long *PowerHike*, you have experienced a new Paris arrondissement and walked about 3 miles. While you are in the elegant 8th arrondissement, you might want to *PowerHike*

a little further along avenue Hoche in

the direction of the

Arc de Triomphe.

Once you arrive at

l'Étoile, the spokes

of avenues leading out from the arch,

take avenue Victor Hugo up one

side to place Victor Hugo, and down

the other side back towards l'Étoile

and place Charles De Gaulle. There

are enticing boutiques and charming

restaurants and cafés along the way to

perk your interest.

Take the metro to place Charles De Gaulle and then transfer to Parc de Monceau. Retrace your steps or explore more of the Parisian neighborhoods off the place Charles De Gaulle and the Arc de Triomphe. The *PowerHike* to Parc de Monceau can also be included with les Champs-Élysées, either returning on foot or by metro.